OPEN 2 TRUTH

BY KENNETH E. WILLIAMS JR.

ISBN
978-0-9853371-0-0
Copyright © 2017 by
Kenneth E. Williams Jr.

Published by
Kenneth E. Williams Jr.
Montgomery, AL

Printed in the United States of America
All rights reserved under International Copyright Law. Contents and/or cover may not be reproduced in whole or in part in any form without the written consent of the Author/Publisher.

Dedication

To my Aunt Alberta Madison, you will be missed dearly beyond words. This book I dedicate to you. I know you're joyfully and proudly smiling down. Someday we will accompany each other in light. I love you, Aunt Berta, now and forever.

Content

Forward 6
Acknowledgements 7
Introduction 8
My America 9
By a Thread 9
Black Rose 10
American Genocide 10
Inside Out 11
My Fault 11
Slanted 12
The World's View 12
Hate Won't Stand 13
Misplaced 13
The Best Lie 14
Set It Free 15
Some Extra 15
Mirage of Pleasure 16
Our Representer 16
See Through Me 17
Trash 18
2016 18
My Reflection 19
A Deep Breath 19
Black Bullet 20
2 The Bitter Words 20
Inside the Unhappiness 21
What's a Broken Home 21

The Free Thinkers	22
Dripping Dirt	23
Timeless Sleep	24
Hidden History	25
Boast On Nothing	26
Blind 2 the Creation	27
Cry 2 Heaven	28
Caution Girl	29
Celebrate It	30
Circle of Poison	31
Different	32
Subtract Trust	33
Black	34
2 The Sister	35
A Lost Poet	36
America in the Nude	37
Dreams 4 Ransom	38
Bid 4 Peace	39
Misplaced Passion	40
My First	41
Chased by the Dark	42
A Hidden Walk	43
Alive	43
Stress Since 92	44
Words n Play	45
2 The Fatherless Son	46

Forward

Son of a King

Son of a king, knew that from the start.
The Potters' perfected masterpiece, now rise up
stand and make your mark.
Chin up, chest out confidence lacking not.
Soar high above this world my Phoenix
and Reign over your inheritance
Psalm 68:5 (NIV)
Abba Father said it
and they shall know what it means
you are
"THE SON OF A KING"

Love Mom

Acknowledgements

Acknowledgements
Kenneth E. Williams Jr.

God, I thank you for giving vision and clarity through the dismal times, allowing open doors along the way and blessing me with the right knowledge for the task.

Mrs. Lessie Garcia-Latimore, I thank you for your extended hand through the guidance of this wonderful publishing process.

Mr. Anthony Hill, I thank you for your editing and constructive advice you provided towards this project.

Ms. Hargrove, I also thank you for your time given to editing and the constructive advice you gave towards this project.

Claude J. Collins, Jr., I thank you for bringing my ideal cover to fruition.

Foster Photography of Montgomery, Alabama, I thank you for providing great detail throughout the process of the session.

I thank all for this magnificent journey

Introduction

Throughout life, much wisdom has been imparted, providing me with the knowledge to see the truth in disguise. There were times in my young life when the world appeared foggy in what seemed for most, clear. Experiences from life gave me warmth and cold, leading to the inspiration of my poetry.

My America

I look unto the sky where only then freedom is bestowed upon me.
My feet share the pavement amongst colorful people, though hate has targeted me.
Fifty stars of hate,
where prejudice, discrimination, and no equality
rides the back of me.
The brown and black continue 2 bare the unhealed wounds that are not allowed to close.
A secret of hatred and destruction that's disguised through deceit and lies.
"This is my America."

By a Thread

A thin piece of hope Shrivels away as it dangles,
grasping tightly for life,
all but different in the same shreds
while hanging by a thread.
Souls in thirst for saving,
slowly slipping from the agony of dread,
desperately gripping the lifeless thread.
Now the stretch began 2 a rope
for a more sturdy grip of hope,
releasing all from the edge
who dangle by a thread.

Black Rose

No angelic scent, with absent love.
Darkness swarms the beauty,
while drooping low and shriveling away.
A symbol of romance and love parishes into the wind as agony takes over becoming the black rose.
Pain, sadness, and darkness linger forever.
For a season, we all share the black rose.

American Genocide

Heavy tears weep for another wasted future,
for a blue hand holds the black hand in partnership 2gether forming destruction.
One race perishes blindly as self-hatred squeezes life from one community.
Self-hatred gives permission 2 self-destruction, while blue hands take command of innocent murder.
These are the hands of guilt that spell innocent with black blood.

Inside Out

The skin of great, but 2 a nation
the inside out brings hate.
The skin bleeds racial pain, but 2 a nation
 the inside out is 2 blame.
The skin cries hope, but 2 a nation
the inside out is a joke.
The skin bares pride, but 2 a nation
the inside out begs free of genocide.
"No matter the inside out,
this is the result."

My Fault

Aggression is my fault,
Hate is my fault,
Poverty is my fault,
Wrong is my fault,
Negro is my fault,
Hopelessness is my fault,
Absent father is my fault,
Black is my fault,
1712 was not my fault.

Slanted

The heart cringes
the mind becomes altered
sweat drips 2 a rhythm
the eyes are confused 2 who
the lips speak what the ears hear
the body travels whichever way
the hands comfort each other
objects appear in the distance
for they are non-existing
2 whom is slanted.

The World's View

Billions of eyes all with a different view,
views in which the world is not of the same essence.
Hearts and minds of the world share a little good while
committing a lot of bad, hearts of flames as love
comes in a pinch,
Religion and race bare the identical burden through the
world's view with evil becoming the new justice.
This is a revelation of the new world's view.

Hate Won't Stand

A burning structure that brings destruction for the life inside,
poisoning the vitals with smoke
and with water in the form of forgiveness.
The hate gives endurance 2 the flames,
slowly collapsing the structure that
won't stand.

Misplaced

Trapped and surrounded by unwanted deliberate oppression,
hiding from the hate while searching for the invisible love
that is only heard as a folktale.
The tears of the soul soak the careless,
and the peace dissipates into thin air
while the hands bobble what's left,
constant jealousy roams at the surface,
showing itself through the predators
who search for weak prey…
a world with little space for those who are
misplaced.

The Best Lie

A truth peeking from the back of a lie,
the lie we've all told
a different but same lie that's often sold
2 the minds of the believers from the mouth
of the fitted circumstances,
the best lie that we all depend on
for a little more time;
the best lie that makes everything temporarily fine.
The tip of the tongue becomes bittered with guilt
just before the fiction slip
in a slow flow as the half right of you
lets out a cry,
because the other half told the best
lie.

Set It Free

A caged pain searching for a way to flee
the confined space that grips the incoming pain in place,
becoming a hostage without expression
and the second you tied to inner oppression with
a dark cause and 2 blind 2 see the pain
that screams from inside the soul
set me free.
A freedom hidden from the caged pain while
weighed down by unbroken chains
searching for peace with the key
unlocking the pain 2 set it
free.

Some Extra

A world of nothing less and everything more;
the world of greed where we all share the need
for some extra, the sin that leads us like a dog on a chain,
bringing man 2 all fours with a pimped out soul
for the desire of more,
drowning in the fire of you
a great lost
for some extra.

Mirage of Pleasure

The fetal position of darkness that blinds the soul,
the pitch of a scream that's never told
though loud 2 self,
the screams ignore the loyalty of both vocals
and lungs
failing 2 bring attention 2 distress
for the soul is under constant pressure,
wandering in silence for the pleasure,
the pleasure that quenches the thirst of
the charred heart and tears of blood
caused by the garbage that tramples on the soul,
leaving behind a trail of thorns
is the mirage of pleasure
shown in the display of this literary composition.

Our Representor

An angel who inherited her innocence by God,
given outer flaws of perfection and purity.
A heavenly representor of the family was clear
despite our cloudy approach 2 the gates,
her king gives space 2 an angel who
comes in first place.
"She is our representative"

See Through Me

A new life of purity,
the black son being led in a world bleeding cruelty,
an infant full with innocence blocking the negative
impressions from those all around.
A world that transforms all innocence
upside down.
A once filled shell of hopeful breath
futuristically becomes see-through
caused by life's depletion 2 nothing left,
nothing left of past innocence,
suffering through a drought inherited
from the surrounding weight.
A clear soul,
an imbedded fate in chipped away mold.
The devastated product of a contagious
world cold,
dwelling in the chains of the unfree;
now all shall see through me.

Trash

Thanks for the save when the foes threw hate.
Thanks for the save when family declared the fate.
Thanks for the save when the trap was set with bait.
Thanks for the save when the crooked steps became straight.
Thanks for the save when the end stared at the brain.
Thanks for the save when the rage destroyed in the place of blame.
Thanks for the save when the love turned brash.
God, thanks for taking out the trash.

2016

A hosted party thrown by the open gates of hell.
A forced seat 2 witness.
Hell I see:
Shook the ground beneath all feet.
Darkness preyed on the weak and
peeking from the fear was a frown
as a flaming smile came around
puffing smoke into the lungs of no exit seen,
while taking hostages for 2016.

My Reflection

A World that's flooded by disguise with a variety of tears
traded by different, but similar fears in the torched hearts of
all where my reflection is seen in every kneed soul,
an existence filled with many stories untold: engulfed
pulsating rhythms.
The beat 2 every breath through countless veins
nailed down by the issue that seems 2 be our same,
sharing a collection of heartache we store daily,
giving the never ending connection 2 my reflection.

A Deep Breath

A deep breath taken for life's treacherous terrain,
a terrain that afflicts for the best in shape a great deal of pain.
A deep breath taken for the stumbles and falls;
this is the terrain through life that knows us all.
A deep breath taken for the heavy load we tote,
a deep breath taken in hide and seek for the search of sleep
and lost hope.
A deep breath forever taken.

Black Bullet

A badge of pride 2 take for the ride,
the hunt is on for the orders are wrong,
orders stemmed from hate,
the hate often the blue embrace
seeking out black faces alike,
seen as antlers on the run:
a sport many badges play for fun,
diligently completing the mission
of shooting down all targets of black,
fulfilling orders considered 2 be a success
with more wild black game 2 attack,
led by a thug behind the badge
with a bullet written in
BLACK!

2 The Bitter Words

Turn away the lips where lacerations split the mind
spewed from the whipped words that assault the ears
entering as deceit 2 the predestined foreseen future
attempting the derailing of success on track.
Turn away the expected actions of failure
and careful the steps taken 2 the beginning
for belief of the bitter words
reverse the steps 2 the rearview of
HELL.

Inside the Unhappiness

A place where most dare 2 go,
the burden of discomfort we all know
inside the unhappiness where it don't show.
An invite gives the VIP pass 2 the party of unhappiness,
the one party we all hate.
The unhappiness in our lives that robs us for its space,
a forced internal welcome that has no place
in the life that functions properly if painless,
but inside the package of life is an irritating
pinch that comes with every breath and a stinky stench.
No matter how we choose 2 bribe it,
the ride is always taken inside the unhappiness.

What's a Broken Home

An unsteady foundation
that victimizes the youth,
caving in all around,
leaving them suffocating and stuck;
and though left 2 fail,
the youth struggle through an impossible dig,
lifting the broken pieces from their ambition,
summoning dedication from motivation
while ducking dismal times.

The Free Thinkers

Outside the box is where the mind
gains strength bursting down walls,
the walls of attempted reinforcement
mounted down by the world convenience
through mental manipulation:
the free thinkers of concentration
without anticipation eating away
at the whole world without
leaving a piece of the lie
because some are the
Free Thinkers.

Dripping Dirt

From the beginning was the start of the blood
emerging from gritty dirt,
a messy mixture of thick impurities,
a drop of we,
the misfortune of an internal walk free,
scars external,
though invisible 2 see
in process the blood transforms
through filtration
an impurity of hurt
now slowly dripping dirt
2 purity.

Timeless Sleep

Stiff and abrupt 2 the realm of a
peaceful hum.
A breath of calm,
a heart gaining strength on a creep,
a brain in 2 deep,
an angelic swirl
in the timeless world
ends with a timeless thief in the night.
A pierced peace of paralyzing
darkness consumes the rest
now compressing the chest
replacing warm serenity
with timeless sleep.

Hidden History

Visible
seen invisible
on top 2 bottom
around every turn.
It's shifting 2 the eyes daunting 4
comprehension
misunderstood, 2 our perception.
A walk forever locked,
an excavated guest of only part
and not whole,
a hidden truth left only 2 the steps
taken by history itself.

Boast On Nothing

Boasting on nothing
the simplistic approach
2 a variety of little given for those
dwelling under the shoes
enjoying their outer stance for they
are not considered along with their
neighbors who do not claim what's
across the tracks.
A beautiful bunch picked over,
seen as 2 small 2 enjoy,
so they boast on nothing,
ridding the shame and no hope,
leaving the veil on the outer,
giving a sense of trapped without
freedom for those who boast on
nothing.
A systematic hunger fed with crumbs
given the only freedom
of boasting on nothing.

Blind 2 the Creation

She turns away
from her seed
though she waters it
with her love;
a constant down pour
on stunted growth
she birthed her dead seed
with a bright conscience 2 blind 2 see
what never was;
a seed she didn't understand.
Angry for her broken seed
no apology mustn't be made
2 innocence and no guilt
ignorantly bonding blindly with
something she couldn't feel
4 this was her creation.

Cry 2 Heaven

A tired duct gives no rain
2 the painful drought leaving
behind a puddle of the past;
the black bones cry no more
for they rise as gold ashes into the
heavens presented now as truth seen
departed as truth unseen.

Caution Girl

The illusion of love wrapped
in disaster was the gift given
the cliff at the dead end
of misleading love led by
the condemned perfume
worn by a caution girl.

Celebrate It

Celebrate the time of tight spaces
that is an unusual fit.
Celebrate the wide cracks in the ground
that challenge each step.
Celebrate the rain when cold and wet.
Celebrate the tears for the pain is
a temporary guest.
Celebrate the failure for a lesson
was learned.
Celebrate irreversible life
for freedom comes 2 the pure at heart.
Celebrate the time
because it never
stays behind,
Celebrate it!

Circle of Poison

Each touch approaches from the
closest 2 the heart where the sting
comes near and seldom from afar;
they come with an opposite agenda;
the entire circle of poison
is 2 complete the mission
sliding in darkness
and slipping away the light
that gave the circle unwanted vision,
a swift take away in a sneak attack
invasion of the now stolen peace
accomplishing the complete
mission covertly
by the circle of poison.

Different

Similar attributes as the next
taking similar actions as the rest,
experiencing similar missteps in
the game of life's chest,
and though similar 2 many
the mind is different observed as
complex:
a machine with a variety of hidden
answers that leaves all perplexed
when balanced
and not falling,
the mind display the art
of freedom
for that is what gives each of us
a unique attribute
and whomever releases its full potential
can truly call themselves different.

Subtract Trust

Step with the left and the right,
only this action will provide rich
insight 2 the eyes,
clarity 2 the mind,
and peace 2 the heart
although recklessly most disregard
this art,
naively taking extended hands
from the start,
sadly trotting behind in the dark
subtract trust.

Black

Through suffering in hate is
unknown light.
In the eyes of the opposite is ignorance
4 they are ignorant,
guilty of not seeing the true man
and woman,
continually giving a
false misrepresentation
of the color that
was led into darkness
now blamed 4 their non-creation,
confused 2 the truth of their self-worth
while forced 2 play as an instrument
in their own self-destruction.

2 The Sister

A pretty glare you share
and a smile of many colors;
a strong black woman and a beauty
like no other
a full spirit and a bright star;
that's the beautiful black woman you are
strong and brown;
a sexy black woman who wears the crown,
an inner crown you've hidden all
this time,
you're a true Queen
with a black outermost shine.

A Lost Poet

Take a few steps back while the
worlds in front,
got 2 retrieve the thoughts 2
piece the puzzle,
puzzled by what's ahead;
in view is a lie,
searching for the conscious thoughts
that will set fire 2 the world's mirage
and reveal the truth
2 the inner man;
the never-ending search for a lost poet's
thoughts that's real
encircled by all around fake.

America in the Nude

Division has swarmed the soil of the land and free
hatred has sliced the blood and soul of all;
greed has torn apart true self
and love has been shoved in the past;
politics turn from often forgotten
though blood dwells in us all;
foreign conflict continues 2 squeeze
families of the stars and stripes
while poverty has become less competitive.
We are America in the nude.

Dreams 4 Ransom

Captivating dreams held captive for ransom,
dreams tied and bound,
dreams of the gold path
but no further than a dream
and anxious wait for fruition,
a screaming dream desperate
for the paid reward
2 free light,
freedom from the capture of
blindfold darkness,
a paid ransom for a dream
come true.

Bid 4 Peace

An auction from hell,
a costly bid,
the peace is on display
unfortunately not 2 stay,
many are in need of this magnificent
masterpiece of peace,
so I stare with a sparkle
knowing it's for me.
I leap 2 my feet
now the auction comes 2 a cease,
this is it…
sold!!!
2 the higher bid 4 peace.

Misplaced Passion

Why is the hunger dead?
Why is the hunger misled?
Away from the feast of clinched consciousness,
a bloated stomach,
a hungry vomit,
but who cares?
4 this trash doesn't get recycled:
a whisper and a point,
a quick glance
at society's dying pest,
misplaced passion
only 2 spoil one's own flesh,
choices of what 2 eat,
nothing chosen 4 the weak,
misplaced passion on self
and nothing else
in the wonderful world of misplaced
passion.

My First

My first u were
with a brown tone and natural texture
while sharing love and pain beyond no measure
where did it go?
A broken bond of no repair,
tasteless dissipating love
like a sweet mist in thin air
a continued lie u wear
ripped through my flesh
leaving an internal tear
in blood deep;
false love coming in hot.
My first u were not,
betrayed by a mysterious con
saved before your damage was done.
My broken first
u were.

Chased by the Dark

Chased by the dark seeking light,
a lost soul in search of sight,
the kind that releases pain,
but all is lost
because
darkness is 2 blame.
Chased by the dark,
chased by the dark,
victimizing alone the way,
leaving behind a destructive trace
of obvious bruised marks,
2 all public smiles of pretend
this is the result of chased by the dark
from beginning
2 end.

A Hidden Walk

I don't appear 2 my society.
I don't ask or roll over 2 why the rejection of me…
the hidden walk
I take amongst no man nor woman,
4 I'm hidden and free…
the hidden walk
A shelter from outside trauma,
a nourishment from discouragement,
a blanket from the cold,
shoes of no bare walk
shielded from the shrapnel of the world
inside a journey forever hidden.

Alive

I gasp in desperation 4 positive air,
dazed in a blank stare 2 incoming negativity
that forcefully jerk my foundation,
running breathless and restless in
search of positive air rejecting the
toxins that buries the body slow,
4 I'm a fugitive on the run
and lethargic from the hunt,
so now I hide
never surrendering a life 2 thrive
while surviving 2 stay alive.

Stress Since 92

Moaning in the place of a cry,
cold and ill 2 the world,
umbilical cord cut,
embraced with a soft motherly curl
guilt stamped on my call sign.
I'm home now,
birth into heated dryness,
led 2 deep cracks across the
young body of hope,
still a continuous wait 4 moisture
as the young life evolves
through cramps and brittle bones
of success malnourishment,
similar results on my grounds
where this drought makes its rounds
2 my identical and passes over a
tiny few…
my agonizing stress
since 92.

Words n Play

Beautiful clumped together,
sadness under way,
anger in motion,
words in play,
letters of their own,
a chosen unique bunch
forming a meaningful bond
digging into the ponders of mankind;
these are words in play,
tapping into a variety of emotions
depending on the order in which they appear,
words in play,
for the low of no high choice
this is words in play
for those of no voice.

2 The Fatherless Son

Growing up as male, but no man around, growing up as a boy, but no teacher was found. A woman you were raised by, though a life walk seemed foggy, because no father was around.

Hatred lingered in the heart while looking for a father not knowing where 2 start; a young loss, without found, because no father was around.

So you kept searching with a depleted heart 2 fill an empty void because if not, you felt your soul would be destroyed because no father was around.

The sense of rejection 4 a father was gone; there was nothing you could do now misled and alone, being taught how 2 be a man "hell no" you were 2 learn that on your own because no father was around.

Where was the love in all of this? Thinking you were created from lust without wish because no father was around.

Still you searched down a dark path blinded by lost vision of the truth; hatred was the only setback you were going through because no father was around.

A heart incased by sickness in never-ending time, your fake smile of happiness was an outer non-verbal of fine, but deep inside the agony wasn't lying because no father was around.

Slowly killing yourself, because hate ate you up, slowly killing yourself because rage beat you up, slowly killing yourself, because a father wasn't around, but the truth was always there, and it wasn't going anywhere because your father had been found.

Your true father said he would never leave you nor forsake you. So while you wastefully searched for your earthly father slowly destroying your heart and mind, your Heavenly Father replied, "Son I was here the whole time."

www.ingramcontent.com/pod-product-compliance
Lightning Source LLC
Chambersburg PA
CBHW061303040426
42444CB00010B/2498